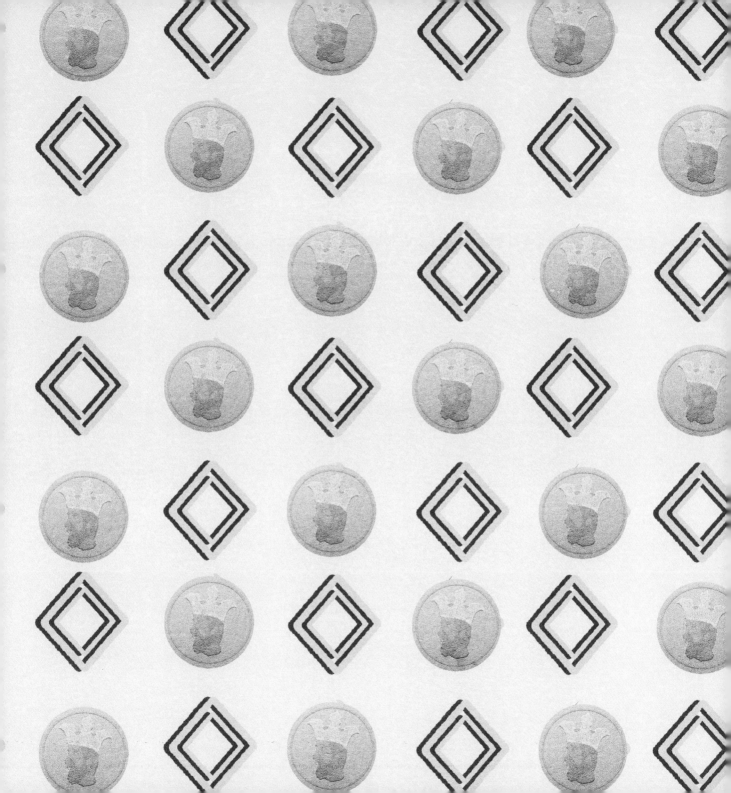

With special thanks to:

Emanuel Colban, Muhammad Muhammad, Juber Hussain, Fatima Farheen Mirza,
Somaiya Khan-Piachaud, Nicholas Piachaud, Eshaan Akbar, Emma Raddatz, George De-Ste-Croix,
Shazia Siddiqui, Sumera Siddiqui, Oakgrove Primary School, Rooks Heath School, Rhys Ravey,
Adnan Vohra, Fatima Vohra, Hamza Farooq and Zayd Farooq.

MANSA MUSA

THE RICHEST MAN IN HISTORY

Created by Our Story Media Group Limited
Illustrated by Emanuel Colban

www.ourstory.media

Contents

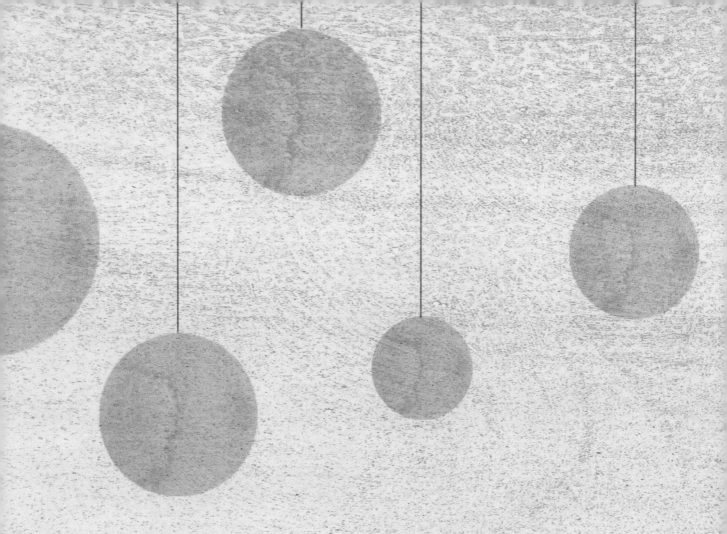

Mansa Musa is the richest person known in history.
He was the Emperor of Mali between 1312 and 1337.

During Mansa Musa's *reign*, the Mali Empire stretched over much of West Africa, including parts of countries such as modern day Mali, Burkina Faso, Chad, The Gambia, Guinea, Mauritania, Niger and Senegal.

The extent of his wealth only became known to the world when he embarked on his epic *pilgrimage* to Makkah, the holy city of the Islamic faith.

Mali Empire

Egypt

Makkah

Africa

Atlantic
Ocean

4

The Mali Empire had an abundance of :

Copper

Salt

Ivory

Nuts

Gold

The empire made its riches through *trading* these resources. It is estimated that more than half of the gold that was circulating around the world at this time originated from the Mali Empire.

In the year 1324, Mansa Musa set off on a 4000 mile journey to perform the *Hajj* pilgrimage in Makkah.

His *caravan* of tens of thousands of people was like a city moving through the desert, with camels, servants and slaves carrying unimaginable amounts of gold.

Along the way, Mansa Musa stopped in Egypt where he met the Sultan, Al Nasir Muhammad.

Together, the Emperor of Mali and the Sultan of Egypt established a strong *diplomatic relationship.*

During the visit, Mansa Musa and his caravan spent their wealth so lavishly, that the value of gold in Egypt *plummeted* for several years.

It is said that Mansa Musa gave the Sultan 50,000 gold *dinars* as a *gesture of goodwill* the first time they met; the Sultan was amazed by the wealth Mansa Musa was travelling with.

14

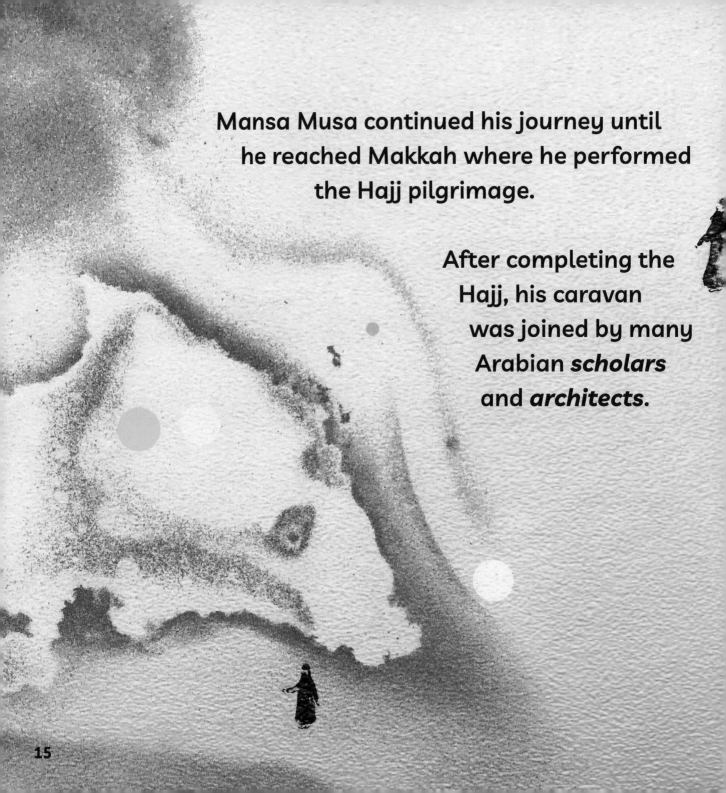

Mansa Musa continued his journey until he reached Makkah where he performed the Hajj pilgrimage.

After completing the Hajj, his caravan was joined by many Arabian *scholars* and *architects*.

$$a^2 + b = b + a^2 \quad + b^2 \quad (a + b) + c = a + (b + c)$$
$$= (a^2$$
$$+ b^3 \quad (a + b) \quad ab$$
$$(a + b) + c = a + (b + c) \quad ab$$

$$(a + b) \, c = ac \cdot b \cdot bc \quad bc$$

$$a^2 - b^2 = (a - b)(a + b)$$
$$a^3 - b^3 = (a - b)(a^2 + ab + b^2)$$
$$a^3 - b^3 = (a - b)(a^2 + ab + b^2)$$

$$a^2 a$$
$$=$$
$$b^{(a+b)} + c \, a^3 \quad a + (b$$
$$+ b) \, c = ac \cdot b \cdot bc$$
$$b^2 = (a - b)(a +$$
$$a^3 - b^3 = (a - b)(a^2$$
$$= (a - b)(a$$

Upon their return to Mali, Mansa Musa *commissioned* the architects to build mosques and educational *institutions* in Timbuktu.

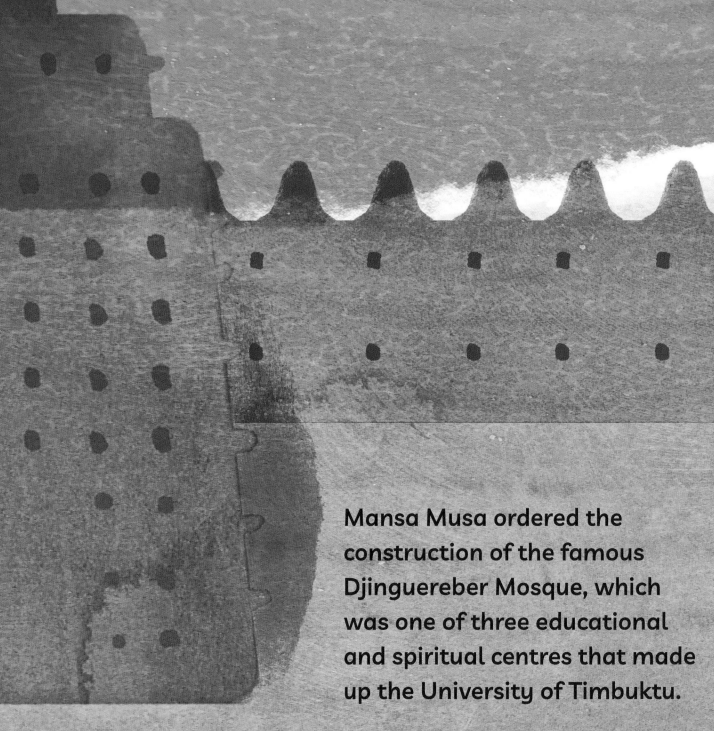

Mansa Musa ordered the construction of the famous Djinguereber Mosque, which was one of three educational and spiritual centres that made up the University of Timbuktu.

The University of Timbuktu attracted students from all over North Africa and the Arabian Gulf; it had one of the largest libraries in the world, housing over 500,000 texts. The education was based on the holy *Qur'an*, the Arabic language and West African languages too.

Mansa Musa saw the connection between religion, diplomacy and scholarship. He used this to build a truly significant and flourishing Empire with the University of Timbuktu at its very heart.

It is remarkable that the richest person who ever lived, a West African King, used his wealth for the benefit of others – would you be willing to do the same?

Mansa Musa

Mali   Emperor

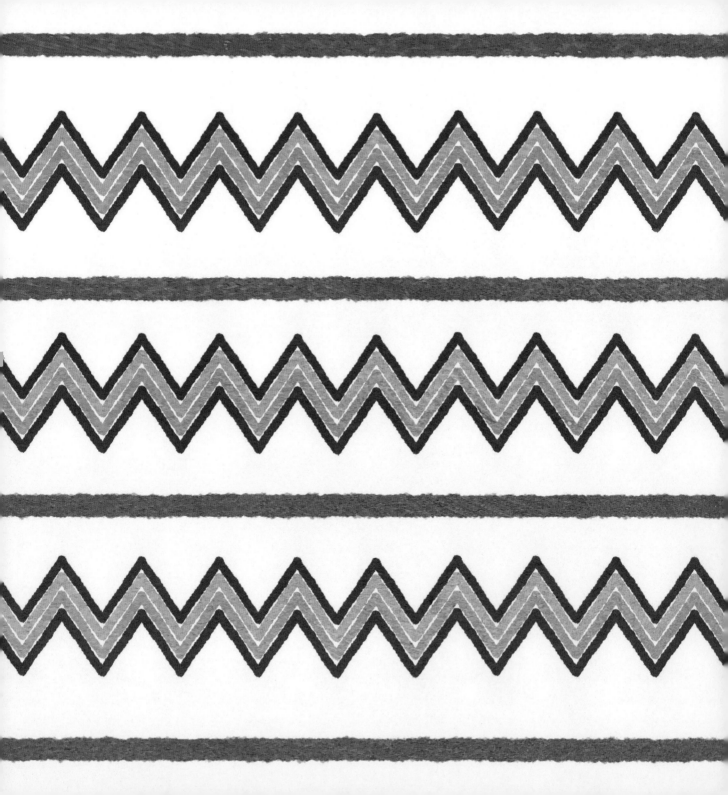

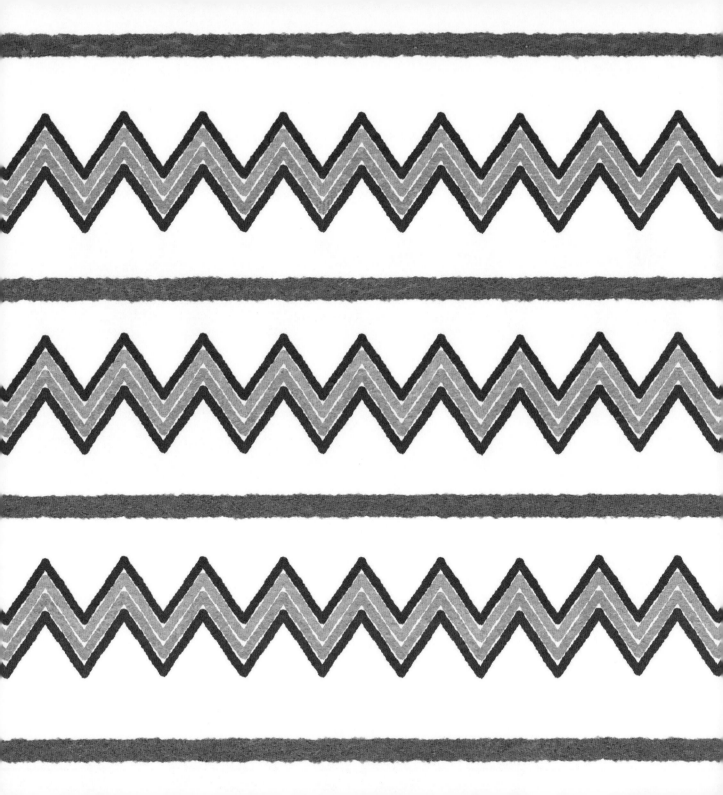

Activities

Go to the start of the book and see if you can work out the answers to these following questions:

How many boats can you spot?
Check pages 3, 4, 5 and 11!

  On pages 13 - 14 how many camels can you find? How many elephants?

On pages 19 – 22 how many trees can you spot in the courtyard of the Djinguereber Mosque?

Check your answers at the bottom of this page.

Discussion Points

If you had all the money in the world what would you spend it on? Why?

Imagine you could go on an epic journey anywhere in the world – where would you go and why?

If you designed your own gold coin what would it look like?

Please share your answers with us using this QR code:

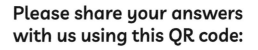

26

Did you know...

How did Mansa Musa become Emperor?

Mansa Musa became the Emperor after his brother, Emperor Abu Bakr II, set off with a fleet of ships to explore the Atlantic Ocean and was never seen again. Mansa Musa was nominated to rule in his brother's absence, and he would go on to leave a great legacy as the Emporer of Mali.

How was he so rich?

Mansa Musa became rich because the Mali Empire had many natural resources that were of great value at the time, such as gold, copper, salt, ivory and nuts.
These resources were desirable for many reasons:

Gold has always been valued as a precious material for its physical qualities and its scarcity. What made Mansa Musa so rich was the huge amount of gold and other resources that could be found in the Mali Empire. Gold was used in trade, and for luxuries such as jewellery and sculptures.

Copper was also used in trade and for making jewellery and sculptures. However, unlike gold, copper had more practical purposes such as for tools, instruments and weapons.

Salt was used to preserve dried meat and to give added taste to food. Although salt was rare in places like Sudan, in parts of Mali it was so common that slabs of rock were used to build homes!

Ivory was used to make knife handles, combs and other intricate items — it is a relatively soft material and can therefore be easily carved.

Nuts are a great source of nutrition. They could be transported easily and stored for long periods of time without becoming spoiled. Even today, Mali has lots of cashew nuts, sesame seeds, gum arabic, groundnuts and shea nuts.

How much money would he have had today?

It is estimated that his net worth today would be somewhere between $400 and $500 billion; however it is diffcult to calculate how much his resources (copper, salt, ivory, nuts and gold) would have been worth in modern times. It is agreed that his wealth was "indescribable".

Did you know...

The act of throwing your *mortarboard* in the air when graduating originated from the University of Timbuktu in Mali, where students would throw their turbans in the air as they received their *diplomas*. This tradition continues today at universities all around the world.

Digital Gallery & Further Information

All of the places mentioned in the book still exist!

Do you want to see what the Djinguerber Mosque looks like today?

Can you imagine what the picture of Mansa Musa from the Spanish map of 1375 looks like?

Would you like to learn about the origins of the Hajj pilgrimage?

Scan the QR code below to find out on the Our Story website:

Glossary

Architect – a person who designs buildings and in many cases supervises their construction.

Caravan – a group of people, especially traders or pilgrims, travelling together across a desert in Asia or North Africa.

Commissioned – an instruction or role given to a person or a group to do a particular piece of work in exchange for payment.

Dehydrated – when the body loses a large amount of water.

Dinars – the monetary unit of certain countries in the Middle East and North Africa.

Diploma – a certificate awarded by an institution to someone who has completed a course they were studying.

Diplomatic relationship – a good relationship between two nations, built on shared interests.

Gesture of goodwill – an act of friendship or being helpful to another person.

Hajj – a journey which all Muslims must make (if they can afford it) at least once in their lifetime to Makkah in Saudi Arabia. The Hajj is one of the five pillars of Islam and millions of Muslims from all over the world still go to Saudi Arabia annually to complete it.

Inedible – is not suitable for eating.

Institutions – an organization founded for a religious, educational, professional or social purpose.

Mortarboard – an academic cap with a stiff, flat, square top and a tassel worn at graduation ceremonies.

Pilgrimage – a journey to a particular place of interest or significance. Often linked to places of religious significance.

Plummeted – to decrease rapidly in value or amount.

Qur'an – the Islamic holy book which Muslims believe to be the word of Allah (God) dictated to the Prophet Muhammad by the Angel Gabriel and written down in Arabic.

Reign – the duration a monarch rules for.

Scholar – a specialist in a particular area of study.

Trading – the action/activity of buying and selling goods and services.

Pronunciation Guide

Some of the words in the story are quite tricky to say so please use this pronunciation guide to help you:

Al Nasir Muhammad – al na-seer mo-hum-mud

Allah – al-lah

Burkina Faso – buh-kee-nuh-fa-sow

Djinguerber – jin-jer-bear

Gambia – gam-bee-uh

Guinea – gi-nee

Makkah – muk-kah

Mali – maa-lee

Mansa Musa – man-suh moo-suh

Mauritania – mo-ruh-tay-nee-uh

Niger – nai-juh

Qur'an – kuhr-aan

Senegal – seh-nuh-gawl

Timbuktu – tim-buhk-too

scan for audio 🔊

38

Our Partnership

92% of girls in sub-Saharan Africa never complete secondary school. Together we can change that.

We are proud to partner with CAMFED (the Campaign for Female Education) to support vulnerable girls in rural communities across Ghana, Malawi, Tanzania, Zambia and Zimbabwe. CAMFED assists these girls to go to school, learn, thrive and become leaders and change makers in their communities, tackling poverty, inequality, injustice and climate change.

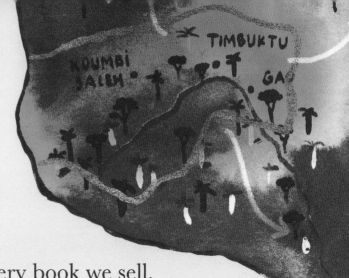

Inspired by CAMFED's work, for every book we sell,
Our Story will donate a day of school to support a girl
in Africa to receive an education and work towards
maximising their potential.

To learn more visit www.camfed.org

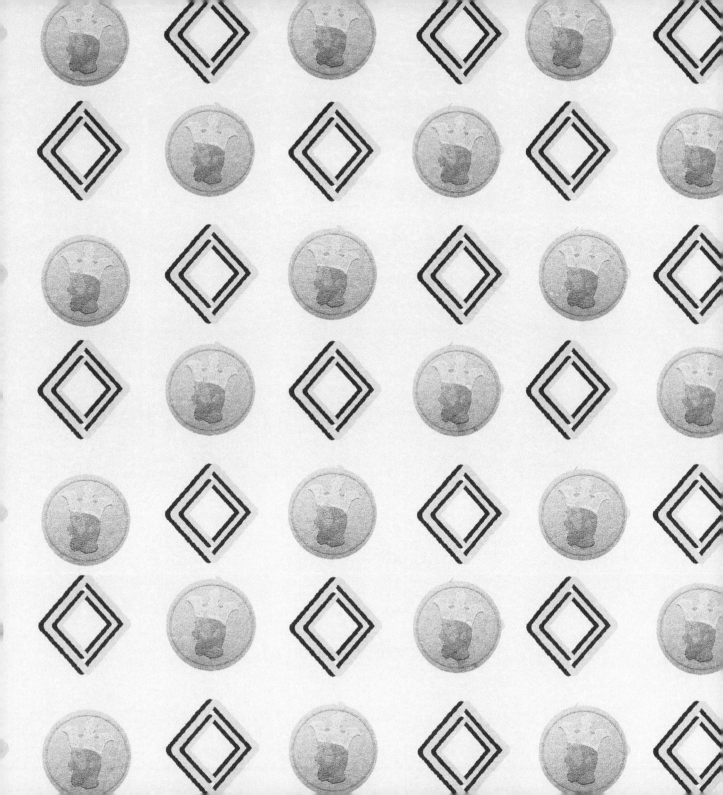

Illustrated by Emanuel Colban
Graphic Design by Juber Hussain

Printed in Great Britain
by Amazon